the dancing phenomenon

KELUCHARAN MOHAPATRA

the dancing phenomenon

KELUCHARAN MOHAPATRA

Text: Sharon Lowen

Photographs: Avinash Pasricha

Lustre Press
Roli Books

A young boy sneaked out during his father's afternoon siesta everyday for three years to learn *Gotipua* dancing. Not that his father, Chintamani, was against traditional arts. He was an accomplished artist himself – excelling as a *pata chitrakar,* and playing the *mrudang* (a percussion instrument) at local temple festivals. But he frowned upon *Gotipua* dance performed by boys dressed as girls, as a vulgar form of entertainment for money, even though it had evolved centuries ago from devotional dance to being performed in the local language in public.

One day the leader of one of the *Gotipua* troupes, Balabhadra Sahu, invited Kelucharan to join the class. Risking his father's wrath, but blessed with his mother's support, he trained for three years. Pandemonium, however, broke out, when the troupe leader asked Kelucharan's father to

Master of theatrical art, Kelucharan's expressions are unmatched.

get the boy's ears pierced and allow his debut performance during Devi Puja. Outraged, Chintamani packed Kelucharan off to a respected and traditional *ras leela* theatre company. 'If he wants to perform, let him learn real acting.' And learn he did!

Kelubabu, as he is respectfully known, thus rose to become the primary architect of the little-known regional dance tradition of Odissi and one of the prime figures in the revival of classical Indian performing arts. Honoured with the Padma Vibhushan, Guru Kelucharan Mohapatra, now in his seventy-fifth year, continues to be the undisputed master performing artist, choreographer, teacher and percussionist of Odissi dance.

The opportunity to work under Mohan Sundar Goswami, the most respected theatre guru of the time, exposed him to fine dramatic acting. Moreover, the legends and mythological tales of Jagannath Puri and Krishna's *Leela* related to him by his father, as they strolled down their village Raghurapur (just outside

Puri), filled his being with creative imagination.

Radha, Krishna, Lalita and other *sakhis* – Kelucharan played them all in his twelve-year apprenticeship, gaining hands-on experience in backstage theatre work, and learning the *pakhawaj* and the tabla on his own initiative. His relationship with his father was, however, destined for conflict. Five years after he had joined the *ras leela* party, he visited his hometown. One day his father caught him with a pack of cards and accused him of being a gambler. The sensitive boy left his paternal home in the dead of night, never to return there while his father was alive. The emotional closeness he shared with his mother did bring him back often, but he stayed with relatives. Kelubabu built a beautiful shrine in Raghurapur in memory of his mother, who lived to be over a hundred years of age.

His oversensitive nature caused him to leave the *ras leela* party and his guru years later. The break was especially poignant because he had served his teacher like a son, without pay, for many years. Defying his guru's censure against cinema, young Kelucharan returned at one a.m. one night from a screening of *Kangan*. He had to face his teacher's ire for disobeying his orders, and because he had the keys to the *almirah* and was thought to be absconding with the contents. Devastated at being accused of theft by his guru, Kelucharan prostrated in *pranam* to him and parted forever.

Unemployed at the age of nineteen, after training in music, dance, and theatre, Kelubabu hit a low point in his life. A frustrating year saw him work as a betel-leaf cultivator, and water carrier for five *annas* a day, and practising *Gopitua* in the evenings. A breakthrough came when a prominent *zamindar* sponsored a month-long religious festival in Cuttack. Kelubabu joined as a drummer, his extraordinary energy and talent winning him accolades. A chance meeting with Kali Charan Patnaik, proprietor of Orissa Theatres, resulted in a drummer's job – his first paying job in the performing arts! He was content with his fate, earning seven rupees per month, plus two *annas* on performance days to play percussion, perform small roles and assist in putting up the sets. One day he came down with high fever. Accused of faking illness, his sense of self-respect made him quit. It was then that destiny propelled him to the last and most important stage of creative training.

1946-1952 were golden years for Kelubabu at the famous Annapurna 'B' Theatre in Cuttack. Starting with a one-month contract as a percussionist, his dancing talent was soon discovered by Guru Pankaj Charan Das of the same company. Pankaj Babu insisted on dance being part of every production, either in the drama or as a prelude. Before long Kelubabu was dancing Nataraja as a soloist and creating his own choreography. While the exhilaration of audience appreciation made his senses soar, he was smitten by the beauty of Laxmipriya, the proprietor's adopted daughter. Kelubabu pined that she was as unattainable as the moon! But luck and his personal charm won the day. Laxmipriya accepted Kelubabu's offering of a single flower! The first woman to dance on the stage in Orissa, she charmed audiences as Mohini, and as a pair they became famous for their duet of *Das Avatar*. They always performed together till their marriage, either dancing as a duo or with him playing percussion.

Odissi's recognition as a classical dance form was due to choreographers and dance gurus experienced in the *Jatra* and *Ras Leela* folk theatre traditions. It progressed from temples and public squares to the stage, with Kelubabu in the forefront. The temple-dance tradition had been strangled by the British Anti-Nautch Act, and though *Gotipua* troupes perform today at folk dance venues, they were not seen on stage until the evolution of Odissi as theatrical art was redefined. Kelubabu learned much from Uday Shankar about training, flexibility, and choreography; as well as Guru Dayal Sharan's usage of Shastric *mudras*.

A scene from the last song of *Geeta Govinda*

Combined with the traditional usage of hand gestures through the *guru-shishya* tradition, he added to his knowledge from temple sculptures, scholars, Sanskrit texts, and even from his young students Sanjukta Panigrahi and Minati Misra.

Kelubabu and Laxmipriya moved to Puri for a couple of years to delve more thoroughly into the *Mahari* and *Gotipua* traditions. Discovery and consolidation resulted in an innovative dance drama on Upendra Bhanja's medieval poetry, with Laxmipriya featuring as Kalavati. In fact, 1953 was the turning point in Kelubabu's life. Moving totally into dance, he joined the pioneer Odissi institution, Kala Vikas Kendra at Cuttack, as teacher and choreographer. Over the next fifteen years, he worked with music composers Balakrishna Das and Bhubaneswar Misra to create most of the standard repertoire of modern-day Odissi. Drawing on his vast knowledge of dance, traditional Oriya painting, temple sculpture, mastery of the *pakhawaj* and years of theatre experience, Kelubabu created an enviable repertoire of solo and group choreography for institutions and private students like Sanjukta Panigrahi, Priyambada Mohanty, Kum Kum Das Mohanty and Minati Misra. Before this period of development, a full performance had been a mere half hour! He took the simple four-minute exposition of *pallavi,* the pure dance theme, with its variations of raga, *tala,* and *nritta,* and systematically evolved sophisticated *pallavis* in ragas Vasanta, Shankara Bharana, Kalyani, Mohana, Saveri, and Arabhi. He merged the folk and tribal dances of Orissa with the poses of temple sculptures in the Odissi dance dramas Panchpuspa, Krushna Gatha, Geet Govinda, Urbashi, Krushna Leela, Sakhigopal, Konark, and Sri Kshetra.

Amazing at assembling things, taking them apart and reassembling them, Kelubabu's skills apply as much to cameras and tape recorders as they do to dance. In the 1970s, he could do perfect editing cuts with simple cassette recorders. These are now done in digital studios!

Kelubabu came to Delhi in 1974-75 to conduct intensive three-month workshops at the

Triveni Kala Sangam for his burgeoning number of students. His teaching methods were unique! In an interview with Bombay Talkies in New York city in 1985, he proudly stated that he had trained 500 students, 50 of whom could dance professionally, while five could take his Odissi anywhere in the world.

The fact is that Kelubabu is both the architect of the neo-classical revival of Odissi and the guru of most of its leading exponents. Along with constant travel, teaching a multitude of students in Calcutta, Bombay, Delhi, and Orissa, and supporting them with his incredible *pakhawaj* accompaniment on stage, the 1980s saw Kelubabu returning to the stage himself. His sinuous lines, perfect proportions and deeply moving dramatic expressions brought life to medieval and

Kelubabu's depiction of Radha is the epitome of grace and fluidity.

divine characters. No one could match the feminine grace of his Radha or the *bhakti* of the boatman from the *Ramayana.*

After being honoured with the Sangeet Natak Academy award in 1966, he also received Madhya Pradesh's Kalidas Award, Assam's Srimanta Sankaradeva Award, and the government of India's Padma Shri, Padma Bhushan, and Padma Vibhushan awards. He has also received accolades from the French Government.

His involvement on stage is absolute. He uses the stage with its potted plants, pillars, and wings effortlessly as the territory of the character he portrays. His electrifying performances in temples are legendary. He not only offers *darshan*; he even receives it himself. Once, in the charged atmosphere of the Sri Sankat Mochan festival in Banaras, Kelubabu became lost in the *bhakti* of Hanuman's character. He snatched off Vibhishan's *mala* of precious gems from Rama's neck, and actually chewed each bead, transformed in his search for

Rama. 'I was so immersed in the character that I didn't feel I was Kelucharan. I felt that I was Hanuman searching for Rama in the beads.'

Examples abound about Kelubabu's impromptu improvisations in a crisis situation. In 1995, performing at the Sanskriti open-air theatre, there was a power failure. 'I indicated to my son Shibu to continue playing the *pakhawaj* and I moved into the audience searching for Krishna by the light of the moon. As the *nayika* Radha, or her *sakhi*, I asked audience members through my dance actions if they had seen him. Still without lights, I returned to the stage, continuing my search for Krishna. Through the arches at the back, I showed the many aspects of the heroine who pines for her beloved. By the time the power came back, I had danced one and a half hours of this single *ashtapadi*.'

The Odissi Research Centre in Bhubaneswar, set up by his senior disciple, Kum Kum Mohanty, induced Kelubabu to shift from Cuttack to Bhubaneswar in the mid-1980s for ten years. At the Institute, Kelubabu made an invaluable contribution to the codification of the Odissi style, resulting in many new compositions, documentary videos and books detailing the new *Shastra*. He immersed himself in teaching master-teachers' classes, along with regular classes. One of his students, Sujata, later married his talented son, Ratikant. After fifty years of teaching in various institutions, Kelubabu and his wife established Srjan, their own dance academy under the direction of Ratikant, who is an accomplished *pakhawaj* accompanist, dancer, and teacher, with Sujata as a principal teacher.

In spite of innumerable honours, hundreds of compositions and fifty ballets, Kelubabu's quest goes on . . . . Halting a class in Cuttack twenty years ago to instruct students to observe my crawling daughter in order to learn how to portray Bal Krishna, or using the *paan*-making

Odissi as a classical dance form, has been taken to new heights by Kelubabu.

process to teach expression, Kelubabu has always taught *abhinaya* by saying: 'Observe and feel, don't mimic or look in a mirror'. The secret of Kelubabu's success lies in hard work, openness to experiment and changing times, and his personal genius as an artist. 'To create a role on stage is a total involvement. Before coming to the stage, I put on my make-up and begin to focus on the role or character, salute my God and guru, and only think of what that character, whether *nayika* or Hanuman, or Kevat, will do. I am already transformed before I enter the stage.'

The stage is transformed into a sacred space when this humble, slightly balding man, with a few missing teeth, sets foot upon it. He holds audiences captive with magical interpretations of an inner world of spiritual beauty and truth. His superlatively moving performances suffused with devotion and artistic dedication, make him a living legend. Audiences clamour to see the divine on stage . . . they are always rewarded with a *darshan.*

■ *Guru Kelucharan Mohapatra draws his strength and inspiration from Lord Jagannath, ruler of the Universe. His home shrine in Cuttack has echoed with his daily prayers and praises, morning and evening, between listening to generations of students practising in the adjoining dance studio.*

■ *Kelubabu gracefully evokes the heroine gazing into her mirror to complete her preparations to meet her beloved, Lord Krishna. This classical Abhisarika pose can be seen in the sculptures of Konarak as well as Mughal miniature paintings.*

■ *Kelubabu as a young man in his early thirties*

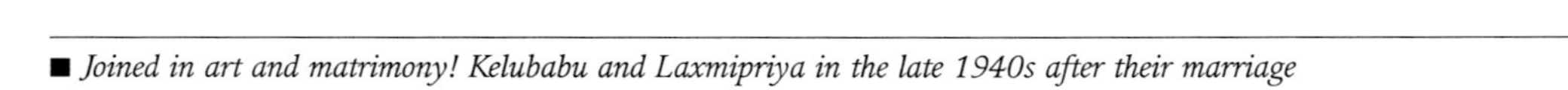

■ *Joined in art and matrimony! Kelubabu and Laxmipriya in the late 1940s after their marriage*

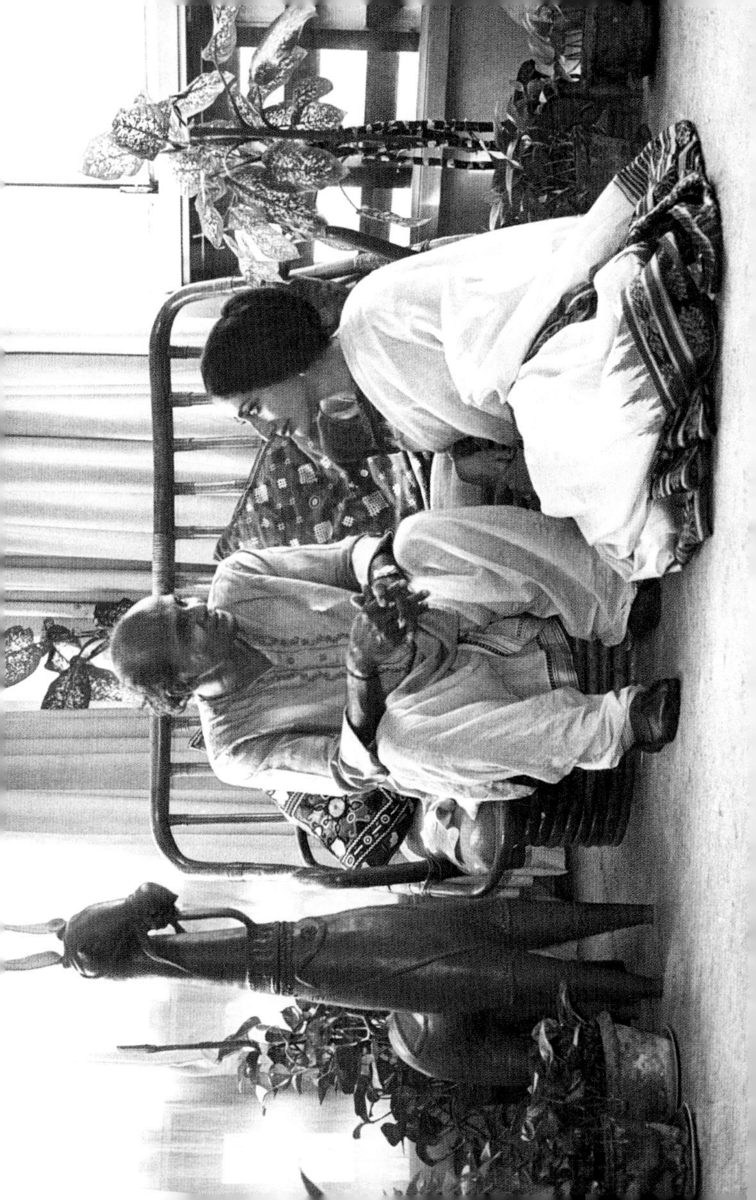

■ *Guru Kelucharan Mohapatra with Sharon Lowen in Calcutta, 1993*

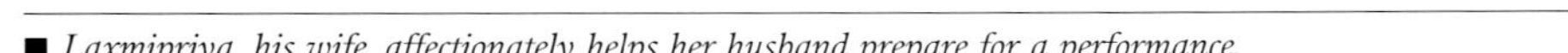

■ *Laxmipriya, his wife, affectionately helps her husband prepare for a performance.*

■ *Kelucharan Mohapatra is unquestionably the finest exponent of the Odissi dance tradition today. The refined sensuality of the form is evoked here as the heroine opens her long tresses.*

■ *Kelucharan Mohapatra has a rare ability to convey graceful femininity while retaining his own masculinity. Here, he expresses the anguish of Radha waiting and yearning for the divine love of Lord Krishna.* Geeta Govinda Ashtapadi, 1993

■ *Kelubabu as Krishna, making excuses to Radha when she accuses him of kissing another. 'It is the juice of blackberries I ate in the forest as I came to meet you, not the* kajal *of another woman's eye make-up on my lips.'* Yahi Madhava *from* Geeta Govinda, 1993

■ *The yearning of the soul for the divine; of Radha for Lord Krishna, is poetically evoked in the metaphor of the* chakora *bird who lives on moonbeams, yearning for the moon to quench its romantic thirst.* 1993

■ *Kelubabu depicts the physical charms of Radha, which she wishes Krishna to acknowledge. The love of Radha and Krishna inspired Jayadev to write his Song of the Cowherd or* Geeta Govinda *in the twelfth century.* Performed in 2001

■ *Krishna appears at dawn after a sleepless night with another* saheli. *Radha is broken hearted and asks him to go. 'Your deceiving words are as painful as the serpent's tooth'.* Yahi Madhava from Geeta Govinda performed by Kelubabu in 1993

■ *Kelubabu as Radha shows Krishna's reaction to her dishevelled state. Her heavy bun of hair has come undone, and Radha asks Krishna to repair the damage in this last song from* Geeta Govinda. Performed in 2001

■ *'The plumage of the peacock is not more beautiful than the flywhisk of hair, banner of love, you must make, Oh joyful Yadav hero, my Krishna.' Radha shows Krishna what she wishes him to do in this concluding* Ashtapadi *from* Geeta Govinda. Performed in 2001

■ *An intimate dance-lecture demonstration shows Kelubabu as Krishna, entreating the Bharatnatyam Abinaya master, Kalanidhi Narayan as Radha, to forgive him in* Yahi Madhava *from* Geeta Govinda. Prasiddha Foundation Jugalbandi Dance Festival, Bangalore, 1998

■ *Elaborate representations of a woman's coiffure are shown with many variations in Kelubabu's evocative choreography.*

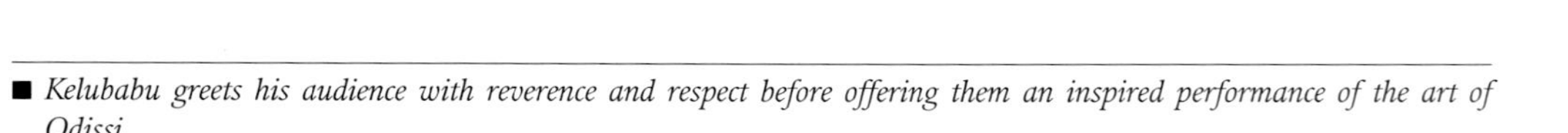

■ *Kelubabu greets his audience with reverence and respect before offering them an inspired performance of the art of Odissi.*

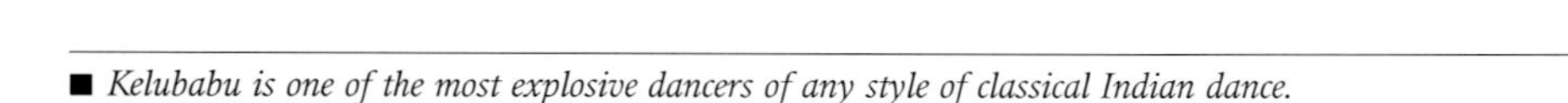

■ *Kelubabu is one of the most explosive dancers of any style of classical Indian dance.*

■ *Krishna embraces Radha. 'Playing to delight her heart' in* Kuru Yadunandana, Geeta Govinda. *The poetry of the* Geeta Govinda *is performed throughout India, but 6.6. were the only verses dared before Lord Jagannath in Puri by the Maharis (Devadasis).*

■ *Kelubabu's performance fills the senses.*

■ *In* Kuru Yadunandana, *the culminating song of Jayadev's classic* Geeta Govinda, *Radha's love for Krishna is fulfilled as she entreats him, the Yadav hero, to delight her heart with more love play.* Kelubabu in a 1981 performance

■ *In 1977, Kelubabu was most renowned as great teacher and brilliant* pakhawaj *accompanist to his disciples who performed his compositions. His reputation as master of the orchestra was soon to be matched by his recognition as the ultimate performer.*

■ *Kelubabu's son, Ratikant, plays the* pakhawaj *for a Radha-Krishna duet with Sanjukta Panigrahi in Switzerland in 1984. Sanjukta's husband Ragunath Panigrahi provides the vocal accompaniment.*

- *Kelucharan is known for his humility and devotion to Lord Jagannath; qualities that shine through his life and art. Playing the violin on the left is late Bhubaneswar Misra, composer of much of today's Odissi repertoire and Kelubabu's main support for music composition.*
- Front cover: *In the power of poetry through dance, Kelubabu speaks to Krishna as his devoted Radha, now triumphant in their union. She requests Krishna to cover her loin with ornaments and cloth after their divine love-play.* Kuru Yadunandana, 2001
- Pages 2-3: *'Oh, Yadav Hero, your hand is cooler than sandal balm on my breast; paint a leaf design with deer musk here on love's ritual vessel!'* Kuru Yadunandana, *Jayadev's* Geeta Govinda